The Prayer of the Mantis

The Prayer of the Mantis

Poems by

Jacob Friesenhahn

© 2025 Jacob Friesenhahn. All rights reserved.
This material may not be reproduced in any form, published,
reprinted, recorded, performed, broadcast,
rewritten, or redistributed without
the explicit permission of Jacob Friesenhahn.
All such actions are strictly prohibited by law.

Cover design by Shay Culligan
Cover image "The Prayer of the Mantis" by Robyn Feeley
Author photo by Jacob Friesenhahn

ISBN: 978-1-63980-716-1

Kelsay Books
502 South 1040 East, A-119
American Fork, Utah 84003
Kelsaybooks.com

Dedication: Patricia Ann Friesenhahn

Acknowledgments

Thank you to my good friends Robyn Feeley, Mark Hansbauer, Suzanne Mobarak, and Catherine Watson for their guidance, encouragement, and inspiration.

Thank you to the following publications, in which versions of these poems previously appeared:

34th PARALLEL MAGAZINE: "Reply to My Great-Great-Grandchildren"
After Happy Hour Review: A Journal of Literature and Art: "rut"
Amethyst Review: "field"
Apocalypse Confidential: "bog bodies"
As Surely As the Sun Literary: "holy saturday"
The Bangalore Review: "agarita"
The Basilisk Tree: An Online Poetry Journal: "The Prayer of the Mantis," "rows," "patience"
The Big Windows Review: "river," "prediction"
Blue Lake Review: "nostalgia"
BOMBFIRE: "Dream of Decapitation," "bed"
The Café Review: "immortality"
Calla Press: "Young Jesus"
Calliope Art & Literary Magazine: "flame"
Canary: A Literary Journal of the Environmental Crisis: "oyamel," "The Naming of the Animals," "tools," "Elafonisi"
Evening Street Review: "grief"
Ginosko Literary Journal: "bright eyes," "The Fallen Ones," "wings," "Losar," "window," "barn," "the dance of flame and moth," "Omphalos"
The Lake Front: News for the Students by the Students: "on limits"
Last Stanza Poetry Journal: "train," "bed"
Litbreak Magazine: "the discovery of dreaming spiders"

Loud Coffee Press: "baby soaks the beans," "wet winter"
Nostalgia Press: "precipitate," "letter"
Réapparition Journal: "black dog," "head"
Rundelania: "bouquet," "presence," "Matryoshka," "footing," "petrichor," "crucifixion," "impossible," "Fog," "Reading Hamann Before Bed"
San Antonio Review: "two grackles," "Bird Island"
Voices de la Luna: A Quarterly Literature and Arts Magazine: "tanagers," "eat," "Pool," "mountain laurel"

Contents

on limits	15
bouquet	16
Young Jesus	17
grief	18
precipitate	19
purr	20
the discovery of dreaming spiders	21
shadow	22
letter	23
the call	24
Dream of Decapitation	25
our first dead	27
black dog	28
bright eyes	30
unforgotten	31
train	32
keys	33
roach	34
Name	35
Repentance	36
transmigration	37
holy saturday	39
The Fallen Ones	40
river	42
presence	43
chimes	44
nostalgia	45
Texas Sunset	46
The Prayer of the Mantis	47
bog bodies	49
wings	50
Losar	51
creek	52

Reply to My Great-Great-Grandchildren	53
morning	54
window	55
November	56
the promise	57
oyamel	58
Flea	60
kite	61
offering	62
nap	63
visions	64
The Naming of the Animals	65
tools	66
barn	67
barbed wire	68
dung	69
lily	70
baby soaks the beans	71
February	72
Cementland	73
Whaling	75
head	76
where it will snow next	78
seeds	79
Gaby	80
nest	82
lighthouse	83
Catfish	84
Selene	85
lost	87
Matryoshka	89
bed	91
tanagers	92

agarita	94
rows	96
the dance of flame and moth	97
Omphalos	98
Murder	99
eat	100
sumac	102
fireworks on TV	103
footing	104
petrichor	105
crucifixion	106
impossible	107
wet winter	109
flame	111
Barranquilla	112
Aelia	113
blister beetles	114
immortality	115
tile	116
Elafonisi	117
wind	119
relic	120
rut	121
anymore	123
secret	124
patience	125
Fog	127
Reading Hamann Before Bed	128
the acting person	129
bed	130
Raven	131
prediction	132
ashes	133

oaks	134
Pool	135
pinecone	136
ripples	137
Time Travel	138
moths	139
bastard cabbage	140
handwriting	141
mountain laurel	142
ground	143
two grackles	144
Bird Island	145
memory	146
May	147
cactus	148
field	149
high tide	150

on limits

if space
is itself
finite
with a border
of its own

what could be
outside
beyond
that boundary?

the outstretched arm
of course
of the creator
no longer content
to stroke his beard

nothing
but the touch
of your mother
every caress
past memory

the impossible
embrace

bouquet

a stranger came
to our front door
holding a bouquet
of weeds
and wildflowers

whatever she found
on her way
whatever had survived
the summer

like a lost bride
she held the flowers up
a spiky vine hung
from her hand

please take these
I picked them for you
please take them inside
put them in a vase with water

they are my gift
for allowing me
onto your property
please
I have no one else
to give them to
and they are not for me

Young Jesus

back beyond
we were already
still not yet
ripe potency
hanging slow
round and fresh
sweet indolence
innocently victorious
before the battle
powerfully unarmed

like young Jesus
before baptism by John
before days and nights
spent in the Judean desert
alone with the Devil
before hot salt winds
arid with temptation
pricked plump cheeks

grief

it was her hands
that told me

it wasn't what
I said
it wasn't the question
I asked
it was so much more
it was everything

they flew to her face
like two frightened
white birds
in trembling flight

as they covered
her face
the backs
of her hands
were weeping eyes
with protruding veins
that ran down
like the tears
I knew
she was crying

the thin creased skin
that covered
those delicate hands
that covered
her face
said everything

precipitate

we fall like acorns on a metal roof
clang after clang can drive you mad
one out of one hundred
might become an oak
dropping acorns of its own

our lives are sent down like spikes
into the soft soil
hard drops in a hurry to reconvene
secretly below the surface
gathering in aquifers purified and distilled
destined to be seen again

we float and drift float and drift
shifting almost horizontally for a season
before settling down on the fall floor
of the still forest
settling down on top of those fallen before
waiting to be gently covered
by others sure to come

our lives are shaken out like a flurry of flakes
furious sugar sprinkled in a sticky storm
each one with a beauty all its own
designed to become one
frozen together in a white blanket
pulled over the curved brown shoulder
of a weary world ready for repose

purr

not a person
or any place
not something
not everything
the vibration
of sound

your old cat purring
as she sleeps on your chest
she's heavy
you like that
purring deeply
levels and layers
beneath
levels and layers
the growl and the whirl of life
the best and the worst

and you know
the sun will rise
in a few hours
there will be time to forget
time for frustration

but for now
your heart beats
lost beneath
her purr

the discovery of dreaming spiders

she feared
the jumping
spiders
were dead
sitting so still
toward the top
of their cage

they are not dead
but only asleep
hanging
by a thread
slightly swaying
lost in sleep
twitching
legs and darting
eyes betraying
dreams unknown
to her

some had nightmares
visions of horror
she could never
imagine
but others
others dreamed
of love
the pinpoint
of a brain
the purest light
held inside
a dark furry body
glowing white
through the night

shadow

I hide in the sweetness
of the shadow
you have yet to cast
I dream of the dreams
I do not know
blessing and curse tremble
in twin absence
from my hollow past
I see the birds who vanish
from my window

I dream of the dreams
I cannot know
dreams cloak me
in their lurid light
I see the birds who never
come to my window
they fly away
before they alight

dreams soak me
in their vivid light
blessing and curse tremble
in twin absence
from my hollow past
they fly away
before they alight
I hide in the sweetness
of the shadow
you have yet to cast

letter

I wrote a letter
to myself
I filled it with kind words
and encouragement

I said we all miss you
we all still love you
we forgive you
for all of your mistakes
old and new

we hope that you are doing well
we hope that you are happy now
wherever you are
whatever you are doing

I even managed to use some humor
and keep it light
and not too long

I wrote it all out by hand
folded the lined paper
into thirds
slipped it into an envelope
sealed
stamped and addressed

sitting on my desk
waiting to be mailed
one day someday soon
from one friend
to another
in need

the call

have you ever
imagined a sound
so clearly
that you could hear it
actually hear it?

your phone ringing
the tired siren
of an ambulance
in the distance

your mother laughing
your father clearing
his throat

and you're hearing it
you're hearing it now

Dream of Decapitation

They look so silly without their heads.
They parade in,
like a gathering of undotted i's,
silent sticks,
missing the o's of open mouths.

They mill about, confused,
probably sleepwalking,
unable to find their seats.
I suspect some are crying.

Everyone I know is here.
No one returns my smile.
Eye contact is impossible,
no matter how often I look up
from my notes—tough crowd.

My friends are hard to recognize.
It has been so long.
No one says, "You still look great!"
I can tell my old lovers
have gained some weight.
None are still pretty in the face.

My enemies look like lost dolls,
lying forgotten in the attic,
their plastic heads popped off—
useless corpora,
ready to be tossed out
with broken green bundles
of tangled Christmas lights,
no longer able to illume.

My sweet mother arrives,
absent in her presence.
She gives comfort, as always,
distinctly without recognition.

The headless are numbly
unnerving in how they stare.
Their necks strain like cut
stems, rotating implied orbs,
globes of empty space,
holding all that is not there.

our first dead

our first dead
bring back
our first loves

they tear open
the heart
in a way
it has never
been torn before

leaving a purple scar
we can only hope
will never heal

black dog

he sleeps with me
under the covers
in the dark
I can feel him
pressing against me
when he shares my bed
I sleep an extra hour

when I lock him out
he watches me
through every window
he spies while I stand
hesitant before the toilet

I find him waiting
at the front door
in the morning
when I'm already late
I find him sleeping
in the shade
of my back porch
through the heat
of Saturday afternoon

he scratches at the door
unrelentingly
it seems easier
to bring him in
he hides under the table
in the kitchen
I lose my appetite
sitting alone
in front of a full plate

I know in the end
he will consume me
but for him to come
so early so often
is cruel

I know I let him
follow me home
many years ago
and made him
my well-fed pet

bright eyes

if I could meet
my younger self
I'd beg for his advice
I'd hope for his approval
I'd ask him questions
then forget to listen
to the answers
I'd wonder if he's not
just better looking
but smarter too

jealousy would get
the best of me
I'd nervously watch
me watching him
mistaking this
for introspection
I'd try to guess what
he could be thinking
I'd end up doing
all of the talking

hoping as he walks away
that was forgiveness
I saw shining
in his bright eyes

unforgotten

where do
the lives
of the lonely
go?

every night
they lie down flat
as unread letters
they wake up
without pockets
in strange homes
with empty closets
and missing mirrors

who laughs their dreams
stamps their hearts
eats their fears?

so much seen
unheard unspoken
so much to be
felt by one
a life untold
unforgotten

train

the passing train
in the trees at night
sounds like soft music

the fan chops the air
in a clumsy rhythm

I sleep on the floor
my eyes half open
I feel reassured
time is going by

taking me maybe
with it
or leaving me
to rest

and you are here
out there
somewhere

and I can almost pray

keys

it was the kind
of keyboard
you might buy
at a yard sale

the clickety clack
clickety clack clack
of the plastic keys
was louder
than the pale notes
that chased behind

his long fingers
enthusiastic and thin
dove deeper
into the forgotten
galloping pop song

I was the only one
sitting in the lobby
of the theater
between shows

with his eyes closed
he cooed
to an imaginary room:

"Do you know
this one?
Do you remember
this one?
Of course, you do . . .
Of course, you do . . ."

roach

when you see a roach
flat on its back
on a white tile floor
its dark spindly legs
waving in the air

when a day later
having forgotten it
you see that same roach
with those same legs
still waving

albeit more slowly now
as if subtlety swimming
away from the ceiling

you glimpse the tenacity
of life and the cruelty
of living it

the battle between
what and that
how they fight
without any why or who
meditating
between the two

the war between
what lives and what exists
the insect and the tile

and the empty
air above
being stirred more
and more slowly

Name

If I knew my name, I would write it down
for you on a napkin, passed and pressed,
to be folded, put in your pocket, forgotten
for days.

I would give it to you, a secret tattoo,
making you mine and me yours,
our names now married in a rhyme,
sealed together, meant for all time.

If I knew my name, I would whisper it
when you roll over to face the sky
above the oak outside our window,
when your eyes begin to close,
when your thoughts begin to melt
into dreams.

I would sign it at the end of this strange letter
in my schoolboy cursive, an almost unbroken
chain below words all about me and me and you
and the truths we held till they flew
from our hands.

Repentance

No.

I am not asking
for any mercy.
I pray no gods
grant me rest.

No.

I am not waiting
for your forgiveness,
to tell me at last
I am only myself
once again.

No.

Redemption
will find me still
where I am.

transmigration

we lie on our backs
side by side
we look up and stare
we are outside
lying in the grass
we gaze at stars
shining invisibly

we have fallen fast
too stunned to remember
what just happened
so suddenly we returned
from our night flight

we are not touching
we are breathing in harmony
we are not talking
breathing *what a trip that was . . .*
we are not moving

sojourners
seeking escape
strangers
lost in exile
which direction
is home?

animals
tasting the sky
beasts who see
past the clouds
angels
tasting flesh
lying naked
on folded wings

looking up
together
saying nothing

holy saturday

to live this way forever
would be torture
what you want is to die
temporarily

long enough for life to miss you
to wonder where you've gone
to notice the singular emptiness

long enough for you to miss life
family and friends first
then one by one every enemy
down to the worst

to die and be dead
long enough for life to disperse
amplifying your virtues
rendering your vices vague

to die and hide under the earth
long enough for life to forgive you
long enough for you to forgive life
and to want it all over again

to die
just temporarily
just long enough
to resurrect

The Fallen Ones

The world was covered in a canopy.
There was fruit for all to eat.
Every creature was bathed in oxygen.

But why did they cut down the trees?
They were thrown down from Heaven.
They wanted some revenge,
to feel for themselves the pleasure
of bringing down what is high.

Now only the stumps remain.
They stand dead and fossilized.
They are the buttes and mesas
of the deserts in which life is scarce.

But why did they cut down the trees?
The great grandfather of Noah,
the wise Enoch who lived by the sun,
who tasted not death but walked with God,
saw them felled one by one.
He mourned the fall of each.

They wanted to starve us
of every type of fruit that grows,
pleases the eye, and is good to eat.

But why did they cut down the trees?
The tree of life was struck at its base,
blow upon blow, until at last even it fell.
Her stump sits, lonely, surrounded by the sea,
later named Cyprus by sailors,
who knew mere echoes of her glory.

The Garden of Eden was not here
on this planet, nor anywhere above.
Our planet was within Eden.
The towering trees were in every land.
One could spend an entire day
walking around a single mighty trunk.

But why did they cut down the trees?
They wanted to choke us,
to cut off the air we breathe,
to suffocate life.

No. It was the sound,
the sound of the singing,
the ancient hymn, the universal song,
of praise and thanksgiving.
The trees would not stop singing.

They whisper still.
Have their tormentors
been washed away?
They dare to hum
to us.

river

there are still
those notes
you can hit

there are still
those lips
that do smile
back

time is softer
than water

all who swim
are bound
to drown

presence

if every creature
is one of her words
is she the author
or the book?

and who and what
are we?
do we live
on her page
or in her heart?

and even before
we were
on her lips
were we
inside her mind
beside all else
that stirs?

when we speak truly
what are our words
if not the echoes
of her thoughts?

and when we are silent
she says what
she really means
and we are

chimes

from my bedroom at night
even with the windows closed
I can hear the sound of the chimes
she hung in the garden years ago

cylinders and triangles
circles of rusted aluminum
once painted green
within the wind
together they ring

like a choir of angels
or the children of angels
as a chorus they sing
about today
and every wonder
I left unfelt

nostalgia

she loves me
for who I was
for what I was
for her

she wishes I could be
that man again somehow
a dusty fantasy
we both know
won't come true

but I was there
standing in the center
with the unmistakable
swagger of youth
when her world
was still enchanted
when we were young
enough to know secrets

her love for me
has turned almost
maternal
her love for me
is less love
than a form
of forgiveness

and for that
I love her more
than I ever did
back then

Texas Sunset

The Texas sun is a restless one,
rolling around his twilight sky,
never sure his day is done,
not yet ready to say goodbye.

The Texas sun sinks softly
in the liquid air,
a glowing red ball
soaked in alcohol,
a bloody cherry at the bottom
of your last glass,

rosy as a drunk face
behind the cigarette smoke
of grimy particulate ash
from a volcano
somewhere in Mexico.

The Texas sun is a dirty son of a gun,
warming the sky just before dark
with summer lust,
still hot enough even after dusk
to make us sweat, as we have some fun,
shaded behind plastic blinds.

Every Texas sunset
is its own season
of hope and discontent,
mixing satisfaction with regret.

Every setting sun
is its own Indian summer,
flaming out with passion,
giving us reason
to believe the day's magic
has just begun.

The Prayer of the Mantis

She bows her triangular head
and closes her huge eyes.
She folds her forelegs,
spiked and raptorial,
as she prays:

"I thank you for blessing me
to bring blessings to others.
I thank you for making me
a snake, a hare, a vulture,
and now this green mantis.

"They follow me
to their long-lost homes.
They follow me
to their graves.

"Some say I'm a soothsayer.
To others, I am a queenly bitch.
Some call me a necromancer.

"But you know me
and always have.
You made me as I am
and as I am not."

So the mantis prayed
before her meal this day,
a helpless grasshopper,
still alive.
Prey held by
the same bent hands
from which her prayer
had been offered.

The mantis ate,
beginning with an eye,
munching more slowly
than a beast with his cud.
Hours later there was nothing
left but the glow of dusk,
halo of hunt and thanksgiving.

bog bodies

mummified by moss, preserved in peat wiser than Egypt
beneath the spongy hills of the boglands they sleep
marinating in humic acids and sphagnum, unlucky in life
all-too-lucky in death, an army of one-thousand elect
the bog people: some shot by arrows tipped with rock or bone
some stabbed to death, the curved apertures of their wounds
cruelly smiling, others strangled by ropes and fabrics intact
many naked with their clothes lying neatly folded nearby
like unresurrected christs asleep through centuries of Sundays
one man's furrowed brow remains worried to this day marked
by four rows across his forehead, dug by the plow of time
and pain, Neolithic, Bronze Age or Iron, medieval or Victorian
brothers and sisters now, they dot the land like the shells
of cicadas whose souls have flown out their backs leaving behind
black bodies aflame with red hair, cast aside they remain
incorruptible as saints, martyrs of human suffering that always
looks the same

wings

angels have wings
like birds
they have human
hearts and heads
with the mouths
of mere men
but with their wings
they can journey
up to heaven
and back again

one pair to fly
another to hide
soft eyes
just like yours
made to see
not everything
a lower pair
to cover feet
for walking
nowhere at night
barefoot across clouds
almost yellow
in the moonlight

above and below
they are free
to come and go
an arc of flight
for us to follow
their song means
like angels
birds have wings

Losar

as a boy
he loved the festival
held every winter
among the few times
of the year
in which he was free
to roam the streets
below the monasteries
in which he was held

all of the sculptures
were made of butter
by knives that gently waved
never appearing to cut
by fingertips warm enough
to caress stems
and petals into shape
flowers that glowed
burning with color
fresh in the chill air

suns and moons
rabbits and birds
monkeys and elephants
wildly alive
lining curved roads
in a parade of gratitude
for the coming year

creek

down along the creek
spring died young
stones bake bone dry
fall forgot to come

the air is so hot
I can taste it
I spit
I stare up at the sky

till it blinks
in and
out
keeping jagged
time
with my jumping
heart

some sage remains
in and among the cacti
decorated by the highway
with tattered plastic bags
waving to me to walk
closer to the border

Reply to My Great-Great-Grandchildren

You may be wondering by now why you don't exist.
I will grant that this is a fair question. After all, the great-great-
grandchildren of lesser men surround you. Their offspring find it
all too easy to exist, as such people always do.

And so you dare to ask me proleptically, your most venerable
great-great-grandfather, what exactly my problem was . . .

as if I have not granted to each and every uncountable one
of you the greatest gift, the gift spoken of by the wise god Silenus,
the gift of never having been born, the gift impossible to give
to anyone but you;

as if with a population surpassing 8 billion, there is any reason
for more human beings, more of us must be the last thing
our poor planet needs.

Maybe I was thinking of collapsing biodiversity, the sadness
of this dying globe, the fun of reading new books at night,
of arguing with no one because we're lost again,
because we can't decide where to eat.

Yet you ask me if I were simply scared . . . simply too *scared* . . .
You damn brats, of course I was.

morning

I drink whiskey in the morning
it washes down bacon and eggs

I drink coffee before bed
I dream of blackness so bright
it blinds me

when I awake I discover
it is already yesterday

and I am gone
and you are here
alone with me

and we are so lost
in love

window

when you are alone
sitting in your car
waiting
while it rains
those aren't tears
they're on the other
side of the glass
of course
you know this

but those raindrops slowly
sliding down the window
so close
to your face
feel like they belong
to you
like the sky knew
you needed to cry
and decided to do it
for you

and look at you
you're crying too

November

yellow November arrives in fog
turning the trees to black and gray
skulls hang like frostbitten fruit
among leaves that are not there
among leaves already fallen

skulls sink into cold caliche
like lost tombstones
they mark the hard earth
outside I wait
and listen:

>   no birds at play
>   no wings to stir the air
>   no insects to sing us
>   through the night
>   no words
>   from you today

I have a heart
like Calvary
from this hill
you have turned away

I have a soul
still as Golgotha
from this hill
you have walked away

the promise

I dance by myself

I dance with the skeleton
        of this room
the bones of this place
        are still strong
        enough to hold

I dance slowly
        like a houseplant
        in autumn
the frosted light coming in
        through the window warm
        enough to glaze
        pale gooseflesh

I sway imperceptibly
        as a girl standing
        alone in a painting
she watches me silently
        from her place on the wall
        she trusts me when I tell her
        soon there must be
        more to come

oyamel

they seem too delicate
to travel so far
an impossible journey
made annually
they arrive tattered
with stories to tell
with wings frayed
like torn lace
of black and gold

many were smashed
and shattered
on our paved roads
somehow a few
still look healthy
some loitered too
long in Texas
only to perish
in the first freeze

near the beginning
of every November
monarchs drift
like orange leaves
down into Mexico
like the souls of our dead
they must fly in search of
a safe place to go

finally they find us
they mate and feed
they rest
among the milkweed
today I watch them
floating in my garden
while I sip hot tea
I have all afternoon
finally they are here
and I know soon
they must leave

Flea

For Feuerbach it was a flea.
One unexpected bite was enough for him.
With a start, his praying hands
flew apart, never to meet again.

But what about the flea?
I wonder if he would agree
with our sad induction.
Perhaps he was only offering
a prayer of his own.

kite

I lie down
I close my eyes
I breathe
slowly
I give in

and it begins
the feel of a tug
somewhere within
the tingling
that intensifies
as the mind opens
something inside
tries to arise
though anchored
below

like a little boy
flying a kite
he knows
not to let go
he knows
he might

offering

they can just up
and die on you
your favorite hen
old dogs
and honest men
household gods
with painted faces
with arms and hands
both wide open

in the morning
you might find
none are still around
to serve
obey or pet
to offer a bowl
of milk
or the whisper
of a secret

nap

you love listening to the rain
        while you lie in bed imagining
secret snowfall covering everything
        sirens of all kinds wondering where
they are going to burning buildings
        heart attacks and burglaries they might
arrive in time for the apocalypse outside
        the beasts and the dragon and the whore
of Babylon gathered together to celebrate
        Armageddon as you keep watch or fall
asleep whichever comes before the crimes
        that must be happening now in this city
that no one bothers to report because life
        is crime and the raindrops tap beautifully
on your bedroom window knocking for you
        not to let them in under the covers warm
and dry you stretch your timeless body

visions

but what exactly
do I want to see?
bright lights
in the night sky?
little beings
with big black eyes
gathered solemnly
around my bed?

the Virgin Mother
hovering overhead
blessing all
her children below?
the face of God
fiery eyes aglow
shining in divine glory
hair white as snow?

and if I saw all of this
all of this and more
would it be as sweet
as the soft soil
beneath my feet?

The Naming of the Animals

I don't know why, but I look
long enough to know what:

the black and gray rings
of a raccoon,
the shaggy fur
of a dog
sometimes wearing a collar,
the athletic body struck stiff
of a deer,
the pointed ears usually alert
of an unlucky feline.

But sometimes identification fails
in the seconds it takes to pass.

But what were you?
Who were you when walking, running,
turning, not expecting to collide?

All inside out and red
and orange and white,
but what name did you hear
from the mouth of Adam,
when you were first drawn,
painted into existence?

I want to say that name.

tools

against the wall
the grubbing hoe
and shovel lean
with a pitchfork
between

the feel of the ridges
in the warped wood
the metal rusted
beyond hope
but solid

steel always becomes
slow burning sepia
hickory or ash ends up
a certain shade of gray
the gray
of the wood
of old tools

they look at you
from their dusty corner
of the garage
they know work
and earth and sweat
and the inevitable
thorn and thistle

they are smooth and hard
as calloused hands
worn to know
how to hold them

barn

I went out and saw what my father had done
        inside the barn he had stacked the books
of his mother books about the insane and
        being saved books about barbed wire and
the angels about Saint Michael and Stalin
        about all of the saints and Hitler and Satan
thick hardback books heavy as black bricks
        with gilded edges with brightly colored ribbons
caked with dirt and clay and the chalky nests
        of mud daubers books stacked hundreds of feet
high reaching toward the vault of the ceiling
        books waiting within to be recovered to be found
before the rain seeps in before the barn decays
        like a wooden coffin and all pages become one

barbed wire

old barbed wire
turns brown
dark brown
powdery brown

a brown that comes off
onto your hands
a brown that stains
your blue jeans

that same wire
older than you
might imagine
can open
your young skin
filling your blood
with poison

dung

I move coyote dung
from the gravel road
to the asparagus patch
I arrange it around the stalks

I hope the stand will reseed
and in a couple of years
there will be enough to harvest

I hope the rabbit discovers
something new to eat
and isn't eaten by the coyotes
those mysterious dogs
who yelp and cry at night

I pray they can survive
on whatever else there is to hunt
between the highway and the creek
and there will be more dung
to find for the garden

lily

as she walked her body jostled
softly beneath her cotton dress
she was holding a single lily
I did not look up all the way
as we passed in the park
I did not see her smile

but the sun was in her hair
and the corners of her mouth
teased the still summer air
they told me she could smile
whenever she wanted
they told me she could smile
without smiling

I try to smile
long after she has gone
my mouth falls into a wince
I try until my eyes cry
with an innocence
of their own

I look back at the empty trail
expecting her to be there
still walking
still holding her lily

baby soaks the beans

the beans were in her pot
soaking in two inches of broth
saturated with coarse kosher salt
her pot was held in her hand
as she danced and danced
and danced . . .

inside a greased skillet
for twelve straight hours
her dress fanned the flames
as she kicked off her shoes
her little toes kept cool
with the grace of a dervish
and I couldn't help but muse:

if the beans are held
by the pot
and the pot is held
by my baby
and she is held
by the skillet
her circular cast iron
dance floor
all the night long

then why is my tea
full of ice cubes
why does she love me
when is dinner
and who's bringing
the cornbread?

February

a sudden change in weather
can cause pain
an old injury you believed
to have healed
hurts you again

chronic conditions we have
taught ourselves to ignore
break back into consciousness

my old neck now knows
somewhere between C5 and C6
when it is going to snow

my left ankle sprained
just off the driveway
of my childhood home
over thirty years ago
stings when the air
turns cold

and when it won't stop
raining my hollow
chest reminds me
the worst of winter
has returned
and you leave me
and you do not
come back

Cementland

Michelangelo saw it all on the side of the road
        the Virgin Mother holding the body of her son
who had sacrificed his life for our redemption
        "How much," he asked, "for that block of marble?"
"What? That? Please, just take it, it's in my way"
        once she was complete Michelangelo returned
to show the old shop-owner what had been lying
        in the weeds across from his shop all along

        so near to death, so far from God
        pleasure is the poison, pain not so
        perfectly understood

the insane geologist with his hammer attacked
        her on Pentecost severing an arm, her nose, and
even an eyelid, brave Cassilly on his honeymoon
        grabbed the man by his beard and they wrestled
till they fell into the crowd of screaming Italians
        the madman proclaimed: "I am Jesus Christ! I have
risen from the dead!" onlookers scooped up precious
        pieces of marble, most of which were not returned

        so near to death, so far from God
        pleasure is the poison, pain not so
        perfectly understood

Cassilly was a sculptor too and the ambitious builder
        of an enormous project full of concrete statues
and obsolete machinery, he called it "Cementland"
        Cassilly's killers tried to make his beating appear
an accident by which the poor man was crushed
        under a bulldozer, but why? on such an isolated
and large complex, why not let the world know? perhaps
        they were not proud of what they had wrought

so near to death, so far from God
pleasure is the poison, pain not so
perfectly understood

Whaling

I picked up the book because I felt sorry for it.
You always find a copy at these used-book sales.
The book was all about whales:
mammals who live in the sea, have hair and teeth,
nurse their young with milk, form societies,
whistle one another's names, adopt the children of others.

Then in one paragraph: whaling became an industry.
Like herds of buffalo, they were tracked
and slaughtered, their migratory paths measured
and traced, so as to better trap the animals.
Thousands of pounds of flesh and meat,
of fat and oil were squeezed from blubber.
The whale was seen as a source of a number
of usable products, cheap industrial products,
able to be extracted from the carcasses of the creatures.
We determined the body of the whale has utility.

And the book was not about whales,
for whaling had become an industry.

head

your heart races away
then throbs
like a hammered thumb
your arms and legs
tingle intensely
lost
to your control
you are shaking
you need
to throw up

your chest
tightens
you can barely
breathe
something
is choking you

you are hot
sweat drips
from every pore
you are cold
chilled
to the core

you are losing
your mind
you are going
insane
you are going
to die

but it's all just
in your head
all of it
in your head
just
in your head

where it will snow next

I want to go
where it will snow next
even though no forecast
says so

and everyone is caught
inside for days
with every road rendered
impassable

with a lit fireplace
and no newspaper
but only a book of poems
about dogs

and I stand close enough
to the window
for my face to feel cold enough
to be relieved by the warmth
of my coffee cup

and my phone is not ringing
because you are not calling
and no letter from you waits
in my mailbox

but I imagine it must
as I take another sip
and watch the snow cover
the top of the empty box

cover the sidewalk leading
to my locked door
cover all the places
on which the prints of my boots
will not appear

seeds

I would like
to imagine
I am still
capable
of some rhythm

and rhyme
maybe even
a measure
of meter
though not now
in this season

of ceding
all that I must
all that I am

not really
seeds planted
too early
seeds purchased
for a price

Gaby

but what did she think
how did she feel
after he gave it
to her?

she was not a prostitute
but after an unlucky bite
by a rabid animal
there were bills to pay
she was a maid
at a nearby brothel
and worked down
at the café
she cleaned up messes
left by others

when she saw it
she fainted right there
out in the street
how did the dirty city
look once she awoke?

before she looked inside
she could feel its rubbery texture
at once soft and firm
wrapped inside newspaper
his blood already staining
the stories of others

was it somehow
any easier now
for him or for her
to listen to the muse
who calls whomever
maid or painter
she might choose?

nest

when birds build
with newspaper
glossy pages
from a magazine
pieces of twine
brightly colored string

among sticks and straw
our artifacts borrow
beauty not before seen

lighthouse

I saw an old photo
of a lighthouse
and I wondered
about the man
who lives there

does he miss
his wife
or has he lived
by himself
his whole life?

when he takes
his meals
on what does he rest
his eyes
before bed each night
who rolls about
in his head
for whom
does he keep the light?

in the morning
what is his first worry
at what times of day
does he pray?
does he find himself
lonely
or only alone?

Catfish

On an early Friday evening
in the second week of Lent,
we sit at a picnic table
covered in baskets of fried catfish.
The gingham table cloth matches
the greasy red plastic of the baskets.

We dip our fingers
into little paper cups
of tartar sauce and cocktail sauce
and of course remoulade
and lots of ketchup
for the French fries
and sour cream and butter
for the baked potatoes.

We drink cold beer,
cheap light beer
in aluminum cans.
We complain and gossip
and laugh.

We are naive enough
to call it "religion."
We are smart enough
to know it's not.
We are wise enough
to know it is.

Selene

I have learned to look up
and give her my questions:

how do you know so much
about our months
our moods
our rising
and falling tides?
are you always facing us
or always looking away?
have we made you ashamed?
what could be going on
on your shadow side?

do you make our lives
possible by drawing away
what seeks to destroy us?
tell me about your parents
the day you were born
are you from us
or we from you?
are you my lover
my little sister
or my mother?
maybe we are twins

how far apart are we?
men may have been
up there
have you ever been
down here?
what are you made of
the same stuff as us
or something else entirely?
are you hollow
or pregnant with ether?

do you circle us?
no
we orbit one
and the same sun
why then do we imagine
you are ours?

lost

I eat alone at old diners
and always tip too much
I cradle my coffee cup
in both hands
trying to absorb its warmth
I stare at the black surface
expecting a pattern to form

I go to churches I trust
to be empty
and sit by myself
in the last pew
an hour later I get up
without having prayed
a word

sometimes I cry
over the death of someone
still alive

I smoke alone on the porch
and look up at the night sky
I imagine it is I who exhale
the clouds softly floating by

I go to museums
almost as empty
as the churches
I gaze until the art
sings to me
I know the lyrics
of every piece by heart
but never sing along

I drive slowly to nowhere
more slowly back home again
I drive until the road's rhythm
rocks me and I forget
what I have forgotten
I stare at the black surface
expecting a pattern to form

Matryoshka

some are harder
to open than others
some act as if
they would rather
be cracked
and ruined
than give up
what is held
inside

within we discover
it is the daughter
who gives birth
to the mother
it is the body
that arises
only from the soul
only for a time
before becoming
a soul of her own

the tiniest little girl
is the only one
who is not hollow
the seed
who alone speaks:

"Hello,
you have found me
once again
in our game
of hide-and-seek.

"Now return me please
to the holy of holies
made by the wooden
wombs of my mothers.

"I am yours
only and always
always and only
in this moment
of play."

bed

since you left
I have slept
on your side
of the bed

when I roll over
it is me
who is missing

my head
strangely absent
from my pillow

tanagers

again this morning
I hear the summer tanagers
on days when I am lucky
I hear their long calls
echoing all afternoon

rarely do I see one
flashing
bright red and small

I remember last winter
and those blackbirds
we saw when driving
through frozen fields
in northern Wisconsin

they would softly
land together
dwell for a moment
then just as softly
rise together

the same flock
seemed to follow us
field after field
mile after mile

forming a dark bruise
upon the land
which would heal itself
only for the wandering
bruise to reappear

in a different place
in a different shape
the same deep black
shining slightly blue

agarita

the agarita do not wait
this year they are already
everywhere

their cheerful yellow flowers
announce spring—some years
before she is ready
they wake up a worn land
abused and weary

but the berries do not know
they grow because they grow
and only know how to grow
in the front circle
in the backyard
up and down the country roads
along every fence line

they grow because gravel roads
still run through some parts of town
because fences made of wood
and barbed wire are still around

lines not meant to last
not meant to be taken too seriously
decorated by red berries
among grayish green leaves
forming stiff and spiky trinities

forgotten medicine hidden
among the mesquite
smiling with bright fruit
sweet and tart as tiny apples

as this afternoon
we eat them
straight from the bush

rows

rows of telephone poles along the highway

crosses running parallel to a Roman road

eyes open or closed looking down from each

rows of homes facing forward numbered neatly

tombstones carved with two dates inevitably

approximate joined together only by a dash

rows of corn and squash and beans three sisters

weeping at the crossroads asking every traveler

if they have seen their lost brothers on the way

rows of tulips purple and red and green brightly

shining under an April sun asking your eyes to

follow lines of life and death and death and life

the dance of flame and moth

the ineffable name
of God is your name
whispered by no one

each one is drawn
to the other
longing to disappear
within

so it begins again
the dance of flame
and moth

consciousness made pure
holding no subject but itself

will you finally
be free?
will you lose
your mind?

eternity never lasts
more than a moment

Omphalos

In Jerusalem gravity is so strong
        the sky sticks to your hair.

Every grain of sand is a star
        fallen as the seed of man.

Time never moves forward
        but spreads out in every direction
        like water spilled from above.

I have returned to tickle the bellybutton
        of the world, to touch what is left
        of the stones, to find a boy in love.

Murder

We saw one of our own
lying dead on the ground
in the middle of the street.

We left our cars, sidewalks,
and shops. Five gathered, then
ten, soon well over two dozen.
We spoke loudly.
We made our voices harsh.

"This is not right!
What happened here?
Who did this?"

We spoke such words
as fiercely as we could
though no one among us
had any answers.

Some stood in place.
Others paced.
An old man started to smoke.
A boy dared to whistle.

Eventually our chorus faded
to a murmur.
We began to dismiss ourselves,
to disperse
beginning with the eldest.

The body was left unburied,
naked, covered only by words
of hate.

eat

naturally squirrels gather
all of the pecans
each and every one
as soon as they fall

wasps taste the figs
not already taken
by mockingbirds

chickens are stolen
by foxes
by coyotes
picked off even
by hawks
some of their eggs
end up in the bellies
of possums

mice chew whatever
they can find in my pantry
from flour to coffee grinds

twice already raccoons
have raided the goldfish
in the antique bathtub
from my grandma's house
now standing in a corner
of my garden

one summer woodpeckers
did a number on mustang grapes
still green on the vine

and tonight you will eat
what is left
what is still fresh
what has not yet been bruised
spoiled or stung
of my heart

sumac

they travel from the Mediterranean
to Europe to the Americas
to add new spice to our pots
creep along among the underbrush
poison us to death
tower ten feet in the air

the sumacs are on fire
up and down my gravel road
scarlet leaves and crimson berries
fruit slightly sticky slightly hairy
flashing forth from the dull gray
of trees lost in sleep

it is the first day of winter
the air is finally cold enough
to feel clean
to tighten the mind
I breathe it in
it gently pinches my lungs
I think I feel better

I wish we could burn
again together
our red flames conjoining
turning blue
pointing up to a sky
still and silent
as ice

fireworks on TV

fireworks on TV
always look sad to me
the colors are never right
the New Year isn't the same
with no one to kiss at night

in July between paychecks
I want to be a patriot
I walk outside
and there they are—
pops and puffs
rising like bright bubbles
in the distance

from the city park
from crumbling
neighborhoods
I suck in the dark
and promise
to keep trying

footing

on my morning walk
I find the footing
of a bridge
that was never built

jutting up nobly
but gently
the modest ruin
of what never was
what had no need
to collapse

its cinder blocks
like hidden honeycomb
the color of its bricks
not a bad match
for this dry riverbed

bricks softening
slowly turning
into powder
worthy to mingle
with dust

petrichor

assuming people must be moving
heavy furniture in the apartment
directly above our own
the weight and the strain
the new combinations

wondering if Zeus and Hera
can still love one another
overhearing your parents
arguing in whispers
about something serious
you think it is you

the sound of other people
having sex
thunder and lightning
while you are asleep

the alphabet
the periodic table
displayed high on the wall
you are meant to look up
in order to understand

what I know is below
the way the air smells
as it begins to rain
the way you start to smile
before I have said anything
before I have discovered
the joke I must tell you

crucifixion

he talked about
the kingdom to come
and the one
right here within
he talked about his father
and the spirit too
but somehow
he forgot to say
I love you

he warned the rich
as best anyone could
he understood the poor
and they understood him
he embraced the sick in body
and in soul too
whoever stood all alone
along the margin
but never once did he say
I love you

he said nothing to Annas
nothing to Caiaphas too
he had no reply for Pilate
didn't care what he might do
even in the dream of Procula
he pronounced not one iota
as he passed through
to no one did he ever say
I love you

impossible

after death
the body so quickly
becomes a thing

of course
the body was already a thing
but a thing that breathed
and spoke
a thing with a smile
a thing that blinked

now the body stiffens
like a penis when one is asleep
turns hard and cold
and green and red
as even blood decomposes

the body bloats
skin breaks
bacteria feast on intestines
heart and brain

you tell me I choke horribly
whenever I sleep
my poor brain thinks I am dying
my heart races to compensate
only to damage itself
to draw death closer

I know none of this
I know only I have napped again
in my favorite chair
I pretend not to believe
when you tell me a celebrity has died
I ask you to repeat the name
No, I say, that's not possible

wet winter

summer ran through fall
trees older than me dropped
leaves and then branches
trees older than me decided
this year was as good as any
to die

we should have a wet winter
according to the man on TV
a wet winter sounds fine to me
time maybe to heal in our homes
time maybe to heal behind books
and coffee

you have been gone long enough
to hate me and to miss me
to love me again or so I dream
we meet in the park
we meet at your new favorite restaurant
we sit down inside a corner booth

the new me falls in love
with the new you
who falls in love
with the new me
our past selves kiss
each other
in celebration

I know nothing like that is coming
but a wet winter would be something
I wouldn't mind

maybe some life would begin
to grow under the ice and snow
maybe my head could rest
and I could breathe at night
and wake to watch the rain falling
slowly as drops of blood

flame

we talked
of old hay barns
we talked
and talked only
of love and life
and family farms
and forgetting
where to begin

you told me
your blood was Italian
your blue eyes flecked
with yellow and green
glowed against
your golden skin
you didn't seem to mind
the shape I was in

we talked
till we talked
no more
we talked and then
you were gone
it was enough
to know kindness
near even now
it was enough
to know one flame
burns within

Barranquilla

You say, "Let me show you
the beauty of my city
full of so many
ugly things.

"You see, the government
is a disaster.
I had to stop watching
the news years ago."

Your eyes are big
and brown
and beautiful.
They invite me in
to whatever is inside.

"You have pretty eyes"
is all I can think to say.

You sigh, "It was through
these eyes that my joy,
mi alegría, left me."

I pray she traces
her way back home.

Aelia

I dream again
of the girl
from the sun

she walks toward me
calls out to me
both hands cupped
around her mouth
she shouts my name
accuses me
of something
truly terrible
though I cannot hear
what it could be

she walks away
with her hands
over her ears
ignoring my cries
my loud promises

too late again
to love her
she returns
to the sun

blister beetles

in the morning
when it was still cool
the side yard was full
of flowers
that were not there
before

they were tall
their blooms reached
almost to my waist
yellow flowers
full of flying bugs
they were orange and
black and swarmed
everywhere

they were not bees
or wasps and did not
seem to bite or sting
when I came into
the kitchen
my hands and knees
were covered
in fat blisters

"Where were you?
What did you get
yourself into?"
they had not felt
the surprise of beauty

by sundown
the blisters were gone
so were the insects
so were the flowers

immortality

the snowy banks of the river shifted
    causing the abandoned cemetery
        beyond the woods to erode
            coffins unearthed
                bobbing to the surface
            appearing oddly light
        tombstones pulled away
    like baby teeth
drawn into the current
    the puzzle of gravestones
        separated from the tombs
            they once pretended to mark
                skeletons floating in sleek boats
            down a river not supposed to be here
        stones etched with letters and numbers
    like the veins of fallen leaves
slipping under the icy water
    the living were unnerved
        the dead could only laugh

tile

the last time I fainted
was in the kitchen
breakfast still hot
on the table
in the middle
of a conversation
with my mother
Where does it hurt?
there was pain
and suffering and stark fear
and the feeling of life itself
being violently yanked
away and the pleasure
of cold tile
hard and reassuring
cold against my arms and
legs and forehead and face
and the pleasure
of sweat pouring
from every pore
like countless open
springs and the pleasure
of being surrounded
of being asked
What is your name?
Who is the president?

Elafonisi

tourists pour in all day now
cars brave as the local
mountain goats climb the hills
there are parking lots everywhere
and a huge new hotel

the pink sand is still here
glowing like a light sunburn
where the sea hits the shore

there are signs now
legislating as best as they can:
You must respect this place
You must not take the sand
back to your homes
where it loses its magic
kept on your mantel in a jar
or forgotten in a drawer

the pink sand is still here
though some say it's not really pink
it's white just like the rest
dyed by pigments squeezed
from the crushed bodies
of organisms too small to see

I have not been here for years
I think of what has been taken
from the one who walks
this beach alone
I pass more tourists
they hold out their phones—
this sand cannot be recorded
sand needs salt and air
water and sun and breeze
to blush in innocence

I kneel slowly
even in my hands
even before it falls
through my fingers
the sand is intangible
it is still here

Citation: Peter H. "Paranormal Blip Podcast," Episode 64—UAP Hearings Fallout, August 1, 2023.

wind

chase him
        and he's your father
your firstborn son
your only heir

chase him
        and he's your lover
dearer to you
than you are
to yourself

one terrible night
you will eat
        the wind
embrace the abyss
kiss the emptiness

slow down
        before you come
too close
to the ghost

relic

there ought to be thirty
out there somewhere
but even he didn't want them
bloodstained as his hands
too unholy for the treasury

he had about as many teeth
all of which are missing
along with his foreskin
he hung himself or maybe
his intestines poured forth
after he tripped and fell

his body was buried
in the Field of Blood
alongside forgotten foreigners
no one clutches dry bones
better left in hell

but he was close enough
to be one of twelve
to question the mission
to know a better way
the location of the garden
where and how to find him

and who are we not to kiss
lips deliciously unclean
that once kissed the cheek
of God?

rut

he's a beautiful animal
effortlessly fat and strong
his rolling muscles held tight
in the bag of his hide
covered in shining fur

the does seem to hate him
he bounces as he trots
his head held down
his ten-pointed horns jutting ahead
he sniffs the ground

they evade him easily
even when he mounts
and thrusts it is only for a moment
they dart away
leaving him on two legs
lurching forward
still trying to hump
staggering like a drunk
descending stairs

in the spring
I see every doe paired
with a fawn or two
they are licking
the white spots spread across
their babies' backs like frosting
they teach them where to sleep
where to find food
when to run

from my front porch
I see one doe alone
in the open field
has she lost her fawn?
was she always too fast
for the patient buck?

I think of the fall
of the last time
you were here
and the air feels wet
with my regret

anymore

you won't talk
to me
or I won't talk
to you
either way
it hurts

once you laughed
at the sound
of my laugh
took delight
in my body
helped me light
my cigarette

to see you
see me
would startle us
both
two animals caught
in twin corners
of the mind's making
backs raised
eyes wide

secret

when I give you
a poem
I tell you
a secret
about myself
I do not know

patience

before I was born
I was a patient man
I waited eons
for something to happen
but who was counting?
not I
not I

not I is what I say
never believing it
all the way

I am patient most days
after suffering
into some truth
your sins make you
more like me

I move away from my past
as a man walks backwards
from a coiled snake

I know to punch holes
in the bottom of the bucket

my skeleton has forgotten
how to host
I hold my breath
bite the insides of my cheeks
crush my tongue in the belief
my head would be happier
with nothing within

I am a patient
willing to suffer anything
so long as it is I
who does the suffering

before I was born
I did not crave
I envied no one
dead or living
I was leaner
than the wind

Fog

I watch the thick fog settle
        into the field scarred by erosion.

A family of skunks parades in
        and out of the garden.
A fat armadillo digs for bugs,
        leaving deep holes behind.

And I can almost believe Rumi:
        my hopeless desire for God
        is already the surest sign.

The crescent moon, curved and thin
        as a fingernail clipping, shines golden
        across the soft back of the fog.

It is chilly and damp,
        time for me to go inside.

Reading Hamann Before Bed

Is it our radical heterogeneity,
a sad world that can never satisfy,
that is the salt whereby we are salted
as sacrifices belonging only to God?

Or when you lick the milk before it drips
from our baby's chin, when we touch one
another within, when we know by smell
we are in love, is not the salt our own,
what is left on our skin after our sweat
has dried like dew under the sun?

Tonight I belong to you.

the acting person

we would go out for coffee
which always gave me gas
the drive back to her apartment
seemed impossibly long

we read Karol Wojtyla together
she had a taste for difficult texts
the actions of a person have an effect
not only on the external world
and on the lives of others
but also on the acting person

she would make pancakes for me
and set out bowls of fruit
the pancakes were too heavy
as I picked through the fruit
she asked:
Do you hate me?

I called her for months
before she picked up the phone
we talked and it felt like healing
it felt like forgiveness
I asked:
Can we talk again tomorrow?

Yes, of course.
       I'd like that.
I'd like it too.

we never spoke again
but I remember the coffee
and the gas
the uncertainty
and the acting person

bed

I sleep with beautiful young men
and women
they keep me warm
though I never touch them

with at least one week's worth
of the newspaper—the dates change
but not the softness of the pages
not the smell of the ink

with glass bottles of water
a bowl of peeled grapes
with a handsome library
the sacred scriptures
of the world's religions
the collected works of Marx
Nietzsche and Freud

in the winter I let my dog
up onto the bed
along with several feral cats
I fill every inch of the mattress
but skeletons and ghosts slip
in under the sheets

they gag my throat
pinch my testicles
as I fight to sleep
they pollute my dreams
with shame and guilt

I close my eyes and pray
to forget them all
to remember the nights
I slept only with you

Raven

We know dove, olive branch, and rainbow,
        but she was first.

She flew across the waters
        but did not brood.
She wondered at the destruction
        but could not abide
        the confines of the ark.
She had no need to see Noah's face again.

So this is the world.
Homes, families, cities under water,
        drown to death,
        the sky still thundering in anger,
        the rain still falling.
So this is the world.

So be it.

prediction

I stopped
and tried to predict
my next apprehension

you
my mother
my father
my childhood
what is gone
what never was
what still could be

wet grass in the morning
movement from wave
to particle
from acorn
to oak tree
from potentiality
to actuality
the inevitability of death

the taste of wine
the smell of garlic
my mind whirling
not as engine
but as transceiver
the breath of the cosmos
filling my lungs
the inevitability of life

yet it delayed itself
hid itself from me
and when it arrived
was nothing like anything

ashes

the Church now permits cremation
did you know that?
so long as the ashes are "interred"
which means a container

a six-sided receptacle
or a cylindrical urn
buried in the ground
or slide into a mausoleum wall
there are different kinds of interment
all require a container

but if we really believed
why not scatter the ashes
across the desert?
why not spread them out
on a mountaintop?
or cast them down
into the sea?

let us show no lack of faith
as we fire our dead from cannons
as we shoot them on rocket ships
back into outer space

oaks

the oaks out front
stand around naked
with their feet in the mud
and hands in the air
they are old men
with nothing to hide

their leaves are still
on the ground
yellow and gold leaves
atop thick black mud
a beautiful patchwork
made not to last

they stand and complain
about the cold
about the passing traffic
and the trash
they mark the border
of what makes sense to me
and what does not

but what do I know?
I remind myself
I'm here to check the mail
I've come too early again
but don't want to go

Pool

After dark, I go into
the garden. I find you
nude among the roses.
I find myself staring
at your glowing body.
A pool of drool
forms at my feet.

You crouch down
to look at your reflection.
You slowly lean forward.
To kiss the surface
of the water? To steal
a drink?

But you fall in headfirst.
Even your sandaled feet
disappear. Who knew
the water was so deep?

Once the ripples calm,
I remove my clothes
and bend over
to look within.
I move closer
but do not see you.

I see only my reflection.
There are new lines
on my face.
I close my eyes
and dive in.

pinecone

when you kiss the silk cap
of the mushroom
washed by rain
when the pinecone glows golden
in the heart
of your brain

more real than reality
beyond imagination

when you arrive to your unknown home
it is your first journey
you have been there before
you have always been here
as you are now
in the sacred space
of the present
the road to which is terror
and fear breaking
open as peace

Citation: "The Joe Rogan Experience," Episode #2091, Guest: Diana Walsh Pasulka, January 24, 2024.

ripples

my oldest memories
      so clear
      so distinct

events that never happened
      never could happen
they occur again
      and again

a persistent irregular
      heartbeat
a handful of pebbles
      tossed inside
ripples bound to collide
      and retreat

Time Travel

They're banning time travel;
    haven't you heard?

We don't need someone sneaking off
    into the future,
    ruining it before we get there.

We don't need people retreating
    into the past, theirs and ours.
Would you want your great-grandfather stabbed
    in the chest before he could meet
    your great-grandmother?

Worse are those who would come down to us,
    invade our space with their phantasms,
interlopers from hidden dimensions,
    manifesting what we do not know,
    all we have yet to discover,
come to stare in judgment
    with those big black eyes,
breaking our laws of physics
    before they disappear . . .

moths

it is not the light so
seductive for your eyes

the sound of air no
longer interrupted
oxygen no
longer drunk down

the silent sound
beyond the static
outside life's hum

or the smell of powdery
wings burnt whole
an offering to the dark
mother of every sun

we tilt our backs toward
what we hope is sky
because only the night
is given us to fly

bastard cabbage

bastard cabbage conquers the lost spaces
    along the highway
    between orange-and-white-striped barrels
    polyethylene tombstones lining broken land
    scarred for now
    for us
chokes out bluebonnets and buttercups
    showing off clusters
    of small yellow flowers
    of its own
shrouds does with long necks turned
    away too late
    now pregnant
    with maggots
blooms brighter than funeral flowers
    ever could
hides pieces of plastic
    crushed cans
    broken glass
takes over early spring
    invading our ugliness
    with bastard beauty

handwriting

the clouds stretch across
the afternoon sky
like Grandma's handwriting

delicate cursive
no longer taught anywhere
words trembling
letters quivering
linked with *Lots of Love,*

I close my eyes and rest
my head in the grass
the ground seems real
enough for me to wonder
all must rise and yield

mountain laurel

the mountain laurel blooms obnoxiously
its fat purple blossoms hang
like bunches of plastic grapes
but I'm not fooled

its cheap perfume pours heavy sticky
too sweet across the grass
down cracked sidewalks
filling the air with an aching haze
a film covering sore eyes
under a dull sun

burning like my tingling heart
that may never know
whether it's really broken this time
or not

blushing like my stubborn lust
for a world full of flowers
among rocks and ruins

ground

we are stalked from birth by the land
        who looks after us
        a worried mother
worried for good reason
        aware of the horrors
        of exile
        of the wickedness
        of spirits uprooted

that mountain
        that one with the cluster
        of flat white stones
        resting in a heap
        toward the top
        is my mother's mother
sometimes I dream of sleeping
        among those white stones
        but I always awake
        to find myself alone

everything that has ever happened here
        ties name to place
        mingles blood with water
        so many arrows
        pin us each
        to the ground

Citation: Keith H. Basso, "'Stalking With Stories': Names, Places, and Moral Narratives Among the Western Apache," Chapter 6, pages 99–137, in *Western Apache Language and Culture: Essays in Linguistic Anthropology*, The University of Arizona Press: Tucson, 1992.

two grackles

I found myself watching two grackles
    in the back parking lot
      pecking at a vomit stain
they would take turns stopping
    and staring back
    at me with mistrust

one grackle looked desperate
the other looked bored
      the desperate one scraped his beak
      impatiently against the asphalt
      the bored one pecked softly at one spot
      after another, as if to say:
           "One ought not expect too much,
           but one never knows if perhaps
           there is something worth tasting
           in this slightly fuzzy pink stain
           before it disappears into the sun . . ."

the bored bird glared at me the hardest
    I tried to smile back
    to tell him I agree
    when a burping diesel engine
    scared both birds away

Bird Island

the egrets have returned
after the pyrotechnics
the screeching and sudden
pops
after the noise cannons
the lasers and the lopping
off of thick branches
after men in hazard suits
stumble about cursing
complaining of the smell

war against white birds
with crowns resting atop
curved necks
every day they fly
to the landfill
to snack on insects
buzzing above garbage

and interfere with aircraft
according to the Air Force
according to the city
and so the rookery must go
the scheduled deferment
of the birds

today on the island
near the bridge
toward the east end
of the lake
the egrets have returned

memory

for Jason Carl Sorley (1984–2015)

he clawed at the painting
like an angry cat
angry but bored
bored but wanting to be seen
and asked to stop

he picked at the night sky
swirling behind Saint Augustine
he mused aloud about what
he could paint over *this*
his supposedly subpar offering

Augustine's sad eyes met his
and he sat back in his chair
his fingernail no longer jabbing
the blackness over the Saint's
left shoulder draped in a red cape

I look into those gentle eyes
and I remember

May

at least I can know
the maternal is good
and vast

an ocean
to be kissed
ground
to be embraced

dark matter
outer space

my head in your lap
your hand on my head

I close both eyes
and am born again
from below

cactus

"like flying butane tanks"
that's what they said in the 1950s
about UFOs

the prickly pear is bursting
with bright yellow flowers
in the aluminum washtub
in front of my tank

the wild cactus transplanted
from the side of the road
to decorate and guard
and ignore the tank
speckled and spotted
with rust and lichen
and moss
no longer so sleek
and white

"like flying butane tanks"
sent by advanced beings
who have mastered
the secret of anti-gravity

do they know the beauty
of fat green paddles
alive with blooms
and spines?

field

I see him standing alone
far away
in the middle of the field
it is getting dark outside

I'm sitting on a stool
in the kitchen
by the window

his shoulders are square
his head slightly bowed
he might be wondering
which direction to run
the irrigation lines

or about his eldest son
and how he is or is not
like him and feeling proud
or a slight sense of shame
pausing to imagine the future

he looks strange by himself
like he could be someone else
anyone softly silhouetted
by a setting sun

high tide

part of me wants to be hugged
        by the moon pulling me to herself
                as the sea rises forming a bulge
        asking me to enter to fall under
the waves to be salted as I disappear

into the distant line of the horizon
        where raining sky meets choppy ocean
                tonight I am content to feel cool waters
        swirling around my ankles as I walk
and walk along this shifting border

feet hungry for the firmness of sand

About the Author

Jacob Friesenhahn teaches Religious Studies and Philosophy at Our Lady of the Lake University in San Antonio. He serves as Program Head for Theology and Spiritual Action and as Lead Faulty for Philosophy.

His poetry has appeared in *After Happy Hour Review, Amethyst Review, The Bangalore Review, The Basilisk Tree, The Big Windows Review, BOMBFIRE, Canary, Ginosko Literary Journal, Last Stanza Poetry Journal, Loud Coffee Press, Nostalgia Press, Rundelania, San Antonio Review,* and *Voices de la Luna,* among others. This is his first book of poems.